The Simple on the Road Cookbook

A Useful Easy, Simple and Budget Conscious Guide for Bachelors and
other Food Preparation and Cooking Challenged People.
Especially if Living in a Confined Space or On The Road.

Copies of this book can be ordered from
www.lulu.com/leftfieldnz

or Bill Rosoman
PO Box 4155 Hamilton East 3247
New Zealand
www.creativekiwis.com

ISBN 978-0-473-16684-7

Table of Contents

About the Author

I lived and worked in Telecommunications, for The Post Office/Telecom and then myself on the East Coast, above Gisborne, of the North Island of New Zealand for 29 years.

A place were food in the wild is abundant, from fish and crayfish to puha, watercress, wild pork, and mountain oysters. The food is fantastic if you are prepared to try new and exciting things.

My favourite East Coast food is Crayfish, Mountain Oysters (Sheep's Balls) and Rotten Corn (Maori Porridge).. Rotten Corn with sugar and cream is delicious though the smell is awful.

From 2002 to the present I have been working, and living in a Mobile Home, in the Hamilton/Waikato and now the Bay of Plenty Regions of New Zealand with many trips in the region and the North Island.

I love food and have a life long interest in Food, Food Preparation and Cooking, since my early days helping my Mother in the kitchen.

However especially since I have been living On The Road in a Mobile Home I have moved to simple and cheap food. I still like to maintain interest and a variety of food that can be prepared quickly, cheaply and with a minimum of fuss and ingredients.

Enjoy

Bill Rosoman Dip CS

May 2010

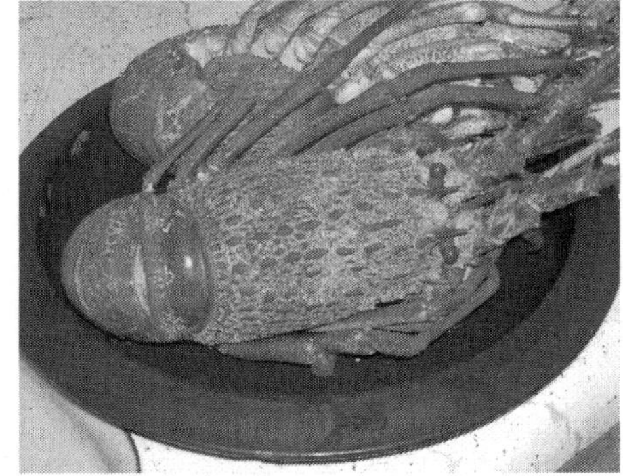

Introduction

A Useful Easy, Simple and Budget Conscious Guide for Bachelors and other Food Preparation/Cooking Challenged People. Especially if Living in a Confined Space or On The Road.

As mentioned I am living in a Mobile Home and on a limited budget.

Currently my Mobile Home is a 1996 Ford Trader I am converting for living in.

My kitchen is very small and my choices of cooking etc. are limited both physically and financially.

I have two 40 watt solar panels on the roof, connected to two deep cycle six volt batteries. I use mains power items like a kitchen Whiz and microwave through a 240v inverter, which on a sunny day gives me enough to do some cooking in the microwave (about ten minutes). I also have a double burner LPG gas ring and a 9KG gas bottle.

I can bake food if I choose, using a convection oven that sits on top of the gas ring. I also have an Aussie Oven to use.

The truck carries 50lt of fresh water and 60lt of waste (grey) water.

The van is fully self contained and I can survive a week or more without having to replenish food or water etc.

I have all the basics of life and for cooking. This book is an attempt to help others in similar situations especially when we are in the middle of a difficult global financial crisis (2010).

I have also created a window garden and can grow things like Lettuce and Tomatoes. I also like the idea and have tried doing Micro-Greens.

Micro-Greens is growing many vegetables like Lettuce, Cabbage, Mustard in small containers in bulk and harvesting and eating the produce when only very small.

My main philosophy is that it needs to be cheap, easy, use few ingredients, and hopefully requires only one pot/pan.

Now that I have my van organised more or less, I buy little in the way of take-aways, mostly because of the cost and the inherent unhealthyness of them. I personally hate McDonald's and things like KFC Chicken have become very expensive. Subway is still cheap ($3.90 for a six inch Sub of the Day) and a good healthy meal.

I just have to keep myself and my mobile home on the road and buy some food to survive. I have little or no accommodation costs (I stay at a camp ground occasionally to refresh myself and supplies), no electricity costs, some communications costs (cell phone, vodem, calling card), and I can even harvest and eat wild foods like watercress and fish (if I ever catch one).

So though times are tough, life is still a beach and you have to cut your cloth to match your income and lifestyle choices.

Lifes a Beach

(Tokomaru Bay NZ)

Acknowledgements

I fully acknowledge the assistance I have obtained from the Internet and good old Google. So some recipes are borrowed from here there and everywhere.

I acknowledge all the trademarks of featured products.

Disclaimer

The author accepts no responsibility for any loss, injury or other circumstances whatsoever arising from the use of information contained in this cook book.

Boys Toys

Well you need some basic toys, like knives, forks, spoons, plates as well as a can opener, potato peeler, egg slice, scissors etc.

Most of my toys are from the recyclers so were very cheap.

You also need a fry pan, microwave, stove or gas cooker.

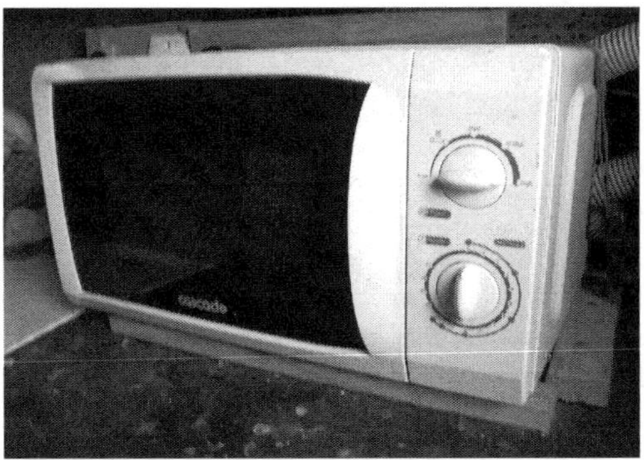

The pantry would be great if you had some self-raising flour, sugar, cocoa, desiccated coconut, rice, pasta, cooking oil, etc..

Some tins of fish, baked beans, spaghetti, tomatoes etc. would also be great.

Basic Cooking Information

This cook book is based on cheap easy meals that take few ingredients and are easy to prepare and cook.

My philosophy is cooking and eating has to be cheap, simple, contain few ingredients, be easy to cook particularly in one pot if possible, and to taste nice.

Marmite is a vegetable extract in Australia they have one called Vegemite. Marmite is great.

Tomato Sauce Americans call Ketchup.
Spring onions = scallions
Cornflour = Cornstarch
1 level tablespoon = 15ml
1 level teaspoon = 5 ml

NB Not all microwaves cook at the same speed. You may find that your recipe may need a few more seconds or minutes of cooking time.

My microwave is a 700 watt model.

Make sure you Wash and dry your hands often.

Wash, dry and put away the dishes as soon as you finish it gets the job done.

All this effort has been done in my mobile home.

So home cooked meals are better, healthier and way cheaper.

So give some of these recipes a spin.

Oven Temperatures

Heat	Degrees F	Degrees C	Gas Mark
Slow	275	140	1
	300	150	2
Medium	325	165	3
	350	180	4
Moderate Hot	375	190	5
	400	200	6
Hot	425	220	7
	450	230	8
Very Hot	475	240	9

Measurement Conversions

Cup	Gram	ounce
¼	50	2
½	100	4
¾	150	6
1	200	8

These measurements are a rough guide.

3 teaspoons = 1 tablespoon
4 tablespoons = ¼ cup
5 tablespoons + 1 teaspoon = 1/3 cup
8 tablespoons = ½ cup
12 tablespoons = ¾ cup

Most of the recipes in this book cost me between $2 and $5 to make, so a lot cheaper than dining out or getting a pizza etc.

The recipes will general feed one person, but can be scaled easily for two or more people.

A two piece pack of KFC chicken is around $7.95.
A pizza is $12-15 at a takeaway.
A restaurant meal is between $15-40 per person at a 2-3 star restaurant.
A coffee is $3-4.

These are the prices in New Zealand in 2010 in $NZ.

Breakfast or Brunch

See also some of the recipes in the Kitchen Whiz section for wonderful Breakfast and Brunch Meals.

Classic Cornflakes

Ingredients

1 cup Cornflakes
1 dessert spoon sultanas or dates
1 kiwi fruit or apple

Method

Cut the kiwi fruit or apple into slices and then put them and the other ingredients into a dessert dish.

Serve with milk or cream.

Porridge

Ingredients

½ cup quick or instant oats/porridge
1 cup water/milk

Optional
diced apple
diced dates
sultanas
brown sugar

Method

Mix ingredients in a bowl.

Microwave 2 minutes, stir, microwave 1 more minute or till cooked.

Or in a saucepan heat till boils then simmer for 1 minute, stirring.

Serve with brown sugar, maple syrup or honey.

Pikelets

Ingredients

1 cup self-raising Flour
1 tablespoon sugar
1 egg
½ cup milk
1 tablespoon melted butter/oil

more butter/oil for fry pan

Method

Put flour into a mixing bowl and add sugar.

Make a well in the centre and add the egg. Add the milk gradually with melted butter, while stirring rapidly with a spoon.

Beat until smooth.

Drop from a dessert spoon onto a lightly greased, heated griddle or fry pan.

When small bubbles appear on surface and underneath is lightly browned, turn over with an egg flip and cook the other side.

Serve hot or cold with honey, or maple syrup, or jam and cream.

Mouse Traps

Ingredients

2 slices bread
some Grated Cheese
some Bacon Bits
1 Onion Sliced

Method

Lightly toast bread.

Then add cheese, onion and bacon bits and grill in an oven till cheese melted and toast is golden brown.

Or Microwave for 1 minute, more or less.

French Toast

Ingredients

2 eggs
4 slices of bread
½ cup of milk
some Cinnamon
1 tablespoon of butter

Optional
Cover in Maple Syrup or Honey.

Method

Break the eggs into a bowl and beat until the yokes are broken. Add all the milk and beat for 30 seconds.

Into a frying pan add the butter and put on low heat.

Dip one slice of bread into the egg mixture so that both sides are well coated.

Add the bread into the frying pan, using an egg slice so you don't burn your fingers. Allow to brown, approx. 30 seconds before carefully turning over.

When the second side has browned remove from the pan onto a clean plate.

Sprinkle with cinnamon, and allow to cool before eating.

Cover with Maple Syrup.

Dip the next slice of bread into the egg mixture and add to the pan as before.

Scones

Ingredients

1 ½ cups self-raising Flour
¼ teaspoon salt
1 tablespoon butter or margarine
1 desert spoon sugar
2 tablespoons sultanas or other filling
½ cup Milk more or less to mix
1 egg

Optional
Could also be dates, cheese, chocolate (cocoa or chocolate buttons)

Method

Put flour and salt into mixing bowl. Add butter or margarine, cut into small pieces, and rub into flour until mixture looks like coarse breadcrumbs. Mix in sultanas or other filling.

Make a hollow centre of flour and mix in enough milk too make a fairly soft dough. Turn the mixture onto a lightly floured board and roll out gently until it is 2cm/ ¾" thick. Cut out into squares and place on a tray.

Microwave 2 minutes, turn the scones over and microwave again for approximately 2 minutes.

Or bake in a moderate oven for round 6-10 minutes till cooked.

These are Date Scones. I forgot the margarine, but they were still tasted great. Makes 10 to 12.

Chocolate Cake in a Mug

Ingredients	**Method**
4 tablespoons self-raising flour 2 tablespoons sugar 2 tablespoons cocoa	In a bowl mix flour, sugar and cocoa, spoon in egg.
1 egg	Pour in milk and oil.
3 tablespoons milk 2 tablespoons cooking oil	Mix well.
Optional	Put mixture into a large cup or mug.
Chocolate Chips, vanilla essence, almond essence.	Microwave for 3-5 minutes.

Muffins

Ingredients

1 cup self-raising flour
1 egg
¼ cup water more less to mix
1 tablespoon sugar
2 tablespoons sultanas

Optional
Replace sultanas with
dates diced
or 1 tablespoon cocoa
or just plain scones with no sultanas etc.
or do not add sugar or sultanas etc. but add
¼ teaspoon salt
½ cup cheese
some parsley
salt and pepper to taste

Method

Mix ingredients in a bowl.

Stir as little as possible.

Place in a microwave tray (see photo below).

Cook 3-5 minutes in Microwave.

Makes 6 (Sorry I ate one)

Omelette

Ingredients

3 eggs
salt and pepper to taste

Optional
Add Cheese, diced Ham, Mushrooms, Fish, etc.
Herbs/Parsley

Method

Beat eggs with fork or whisk in a bowl enough to blend yolks and whites thoroughly.

Add salt and pepper and optional Filling.

Microwave in an Omelette Dish for 2-3 Minutes, turn over and Microwave 2 minutes.

Can also be cooked with oil in a fry pan.

A Nice and Tasty Sardine Omelette.

Baked Beans Supreme

Baked Beans are my favourite food, yum!

Ingredients

1 tin baked beans or spaghetti
1 onion sliced
some cubed sausage, bacon, luncheon
4 slices of toast

Optional
cheese
chives or parsley

Method

Peel onion, place onto a plate with meat, microwave 2-3 minutes.

Open tin beans and place contents onto the plate.

Microwave for 2-3 minutes.

Can also cook in a fry pan.

Peel onion, place onto a fry pan with meat and a small amount of oil, cook 2-3 minutes.

Open tin beans and place contents into the fry pan..

Cook for 2-3 minutes.

Make Toast and Enjoy.

I added some smoked saveloy.

Stuffed Potatoes

Ingredients

2 medium potatoes, washed with skins on.
1 tablespoon milk
1 teaspoon butter/margarine
1 spring onion
some Ham diced
¼ cup grated cheese

Method

Wash and Prick potatoes several times with a fork.

Cook in microwave uncovered for 5 minutes or until tender when pricked with fork.

Gently cut the top of the potato and leave to cool a little for 5 minutes.

Carefully scoop out the potato from the skin, being careful not to break the skin.

Put the scooped out potato into a bowl and mash with the milk and margarine.

Chop spring onion finely, add some chopped ham and half the grated cheese and mix in with the mashed potatoes.

Spoon into the potato skins.

Sprinkle the remaining grated cheese and microwave again for 3 minutes.

Scrambled Eggs

Ingredients	**Method**
2 eggs splash milk salt and pepper to taste knob butter/or a little oil	Mix ingredient in a bowl. Microwave 2 minutes stir and microwave 1 more minute till cooked.
optional small tin tuna sausages baked beans parsley	Or heat a little oil in a fry pan. Add the mixture to the fry pan heat till cooked.

Scrambled eggs and a small tin of tuna with tomato sauce.

Chunky Soup

Ingredients	**Method**
1 tin chunky hearty soup extra vegetables if required, tin of peas	Open can and empty into a bowl and microwave for 2-3 minutes.
Toast	Or empty into a saucepan and heat over a hot ring till hot.
	Serve with toast.

I added some extra smoked saveloy.

Curried Cream of Onion Soup

Ingredients

1 tablespoon butter/margarine
2-4 onions, peeled, sliced and chopped
2 level teaspoons curry powder
½ cup milk
2 tablespoon cream
2 cups water
1 tablespoon chicken stock powder
salt and pepper to taste

Optional
carrots, mixed vegetables, celery

Method

In a bowl melt butter.

In a fry pan add melted butter, onions, and curry powder.

Fry gently for about 5 minutes, stirring to prevent sticking.

In a saucepan add the onions and the other ingredients except the milk and cream, bring to the boil and simmer 25-30 minutes until vegetables cooked.

Add milk and cream, bring to boil for a couple of minutes.

Serve with croutons or toast.

Sweet Food/Desserts

Double Chocolate Biscuits

Ingredients

¼ cup butter/margarine
½ teaspoon vanilla essence
¾ cup self-raising flour
2 tablespoons cocoa
¼ cup chocolate buttons
1-2 tablespoons milk
¼ cup brown sugar

Method

In a bowl cream butter and vanilla together.

Add other ingredients and mix till smooth.

On a plate make 5-6 balls and flatten with a fork.

microwave for 3-5 minutes until firm.

Make another 5-6 balls, flatten and microwave for 3-5 minutes till firm.

Or preheat oven to 230C/450F, mix and roll to 10mm/½ inch thick cut to biscuit rounds and bake for 10 minutes approximately.

Chocolate Brownies

Ingredients

50g/2oz dark cooking chocolate or buttons
100g/4oz butter/margarine softened
1 teaspoon vanilla essence
220g/8oz sugar
2 eggs
50g/2oz self-raising flour
pinch of salt

Optional
sultanas
dates sliced
chocolate icing

Method

Break up the chocolate into a bowl and microwave for 1-2 minutes till melted. Or heat in a saucepan on the stove.

Add other ingredients to the bowl and mix till smooth.

Pour the mixture onto a dish and microwave for 5-8 minutes until firm.

Or preheat oven to 230C/450F, and bake for 20 minutes approximately till cooked

Allow to cool cut into squares.

Serve with chocolate icing.

Chocolate Bread Pudding

Ingredients

2 slices bread
2 tablespoons chocolate chips
½ cup milk
1 egg
1 tablespoon sugar
½ teaspoon nutmeg/cinnamon/vanilla essence
2 tablespoons raisins or sultanas

Method

break up bread into an oven dish or bowl.

Mix other ingredients in a bowl and add to the dish.

Microwave for 3-4 minutes.

Or Bake for 15-20 minutes in moderate oven, more or less.

Apple Pudding

Ingredients

1 apple cored and diced
3 tablespoons golden syrup
½ cup sugar
½ cup butter/margarine
6 tablespoons milk
½ teaspoon baking powder
½ teaspoon cinnamon

Optional Toppings
corn flakes
custard

Method

put golden .syrup and apple in the bottom of a bowl.

Mix other ingredients in another bowl, then add to apples.

Cook in microwave for 3-5 minutes.

Pancakes

Ingredients

1 cup self-raising Flour
1 tablespoon sugar
1 egg
¼ cup milk
1 tablespoons butter/oil, to cook with

Method

put butter/oil into a fry pan and heat.

Mix ingredients in a bowl, use enough milk to make a nice mixture.

Pour small amounts into the fry pan and cook.

When bubbles appear or when it looks ready, flip the Pancake and cook the other side.

Serve with Maple Syrup or Honey.

Healthy Muesli Balls

Ingredients

4 tablespoons peanut butter
½ cup milk powder
¼ cup of dates
¼ cup of sultanas
¼ cup of nuts
1 tablespoon honey
some desiccated coconut for rolling balls in

Method

Mix all the ingredients in a bowl, may need a dash of water to mix well.

Place some desiccated coconut on a board.

Roll the mixture into small balls, covering in desiccated coconut.

Healthy Breakfast Bars

Ingredients

½ cup dry instant oatmeal
2 tablespoons chocolate chips
1 tablespoon peanut butter
2 tablespoons sultanas
1 tablespoon honey
¼ cup milk powder
2 tablespoons of dates

some desiccated coconut for coating bars in
dash of water to mix

Method

Mix all the ingredients in a bowl, may need a
dash of water to mix well.

Form into a square in a tray or on a board, cut
into bars covering in desiccated coconut or icing
sugar.

Marshmallow Balls

Ingredients

100g butter/margarine
2 tablespoons cocoa
½ cup brown sugar
½ tin condensed milk
1 teaspoon vanilla essence
2 cups plain biscuits crushed
10-12 marshmallows cut in half
some desiccated coconut for coating bars in
dash of water to mix

Method

Mix all the ingredients in a bowl, except the marshmallows and coconut, you may need a dash of water to mix well.

With wet hands cover the marshmallows in the mixture and cover in desiccated coconut or icing sugar.

Pavlova

There would be no New Zealander who would not include a Pavlova in their collection.

Lovely with kiwi fruit or strawberries and whipped cream.

Ingredients	**Method**
1 egg white ¾ cup caster sugar 2 tablespoons hot water 1 teaspoon baking powder 1 teaspoon vinegar ½ teaspoon vanilla essence a small pinch of salt Serve with; Kiwi fruit Strawberries Whipped Cream	Separate the egg white into a large Kitchen whiz container. Add half the sugar, then the vinegar, salt and water to the container. Using the small two blade cutter, Beat approximately 1 minute. Add the rest of the sugar and beat for 1 minute until stiff and fluffy. Add in the baking powder and vanilla and mix for ½ minute. Put into a large bowl and let stand for a few minutes. Cook on high for 3-5 minutes in the microwave. Stand for awhile to cool.

Pavlova with Boysenberries.

Whipped Cream

Keep cream cold and use straight from the fridge.

Ideally pour it into a cold metal bowl and beat over a basin of cold water (use ice cubes in hot weather).

Add a teaspoon of vanilla essence and 2 tablespoons of icing sugar.

Beat until stiff, taking care not to over beat or the cream will curdle.

Using a Kitchen Whiz.

Mix ingredients and using the small two blade cutter mix for 30-40 seconds.

Now shake vigorously by hand for 30-40 seconds.

Mix with Kitchen Whiz for 30-40 seconds.

If needed again shake vigorously by hand for 30-40 seconds.

Chocolate Sponge Pudding

Lovely with kiwi fruit or strawberries and whipped cream.

Ingredients

1 cup self raising flour
1 ½ tablespoon cocoa
½ cup sugar
50g butter melted
½ cup milk
1 teaspoon vanilla essence

Topping
¾ cup Nestle Nesquik Chocolate
1 ½ cup hot water

Serve with;
Kiwi fruit
Strawberries
Whipped Cream

Method

Stir the flour, cocoa, melted butter, milk and vanilla essence into a bowl or dish until they are just mixed.

Sprinkle the Nesquik over the top of the mixture.

Carefully pour the hot water over the mixture using the back of a spoon.

Cook on medium for 8-10 minutes in the microwave.

Stand for awhile to cool.

Add fruit and cream and serve.

Snow Drop Rumbles

Ingredients

1 Cup icing sugar
½ Cup sultanas
½ Cup butter/margarine
1 Cup desiccated coconut + a little extra to sprinkle on Rumbles
3 tablespoons cocoa

Optional
shot of Rum.

Method

Place the butter in a bowl, cook 20 seconds in microwave to melt

Combine with the other ingredients.

Add a little water if still too dry, (but easy on the water).

Place some desiccated coconut on a board.

Roll the mixture into small balls, covering in desiccated coconut.

Fruit Cream

Ingredients

¾ cup milk
2 teaspoons sugar
2 teaspoons cornflour
1 egg
1 cup fruit sliced (kiwi fruit, berries, banana)
½ tsp vanilla essence
Cream for topping

Optional
apple, pears, oranges, peaches

Method

Combine milk, cornflour, sugar, egg, vanilla essence in a saucepan.

Cook over medium heat element for a short while.

Or microwave for 2 minutes.

Stir, microwave for 2 minutes or until looking OK.

Fold fruit into custard.

Add Cream for topping.

Sliced Apple and Topping, very nice.

Fudge Cake

Ingredients

1 tin condensed milk
1 cup mixed fruit
1 packet crushed wine (plain tea) biscuits
1 cup desiccated coconut
¼ cup nuts
2 tablespoons cocoa
1 teaspoon vanilla essence

Method

Place all dry ingredients into a bowl.

Add condensed milk and vanilla essence.

Mix well.

Press into a flat bowl/tray.

Cover with some desiccated coconut.

Easy to make and great to eat.

Fresh Fruit Cake

Ingredients

2 tablespoons butter/margarine melted
1 egg
¾ cup self raising flour
½ cup caster sugar
1 cup fresh fruit

Optional
apple, peach, nectarine, berries

Cut down sugar for sweet fruit

Method

Place all ingredients into a bowl.

Mix well.

Cook in microwave for 5 minutes.

Check and if needed cook for 2-3 minutes more.

In an oven, cook in a moderate oven for 25-30 minutes till cooked.

This is a Kiwifruit Cake.

Main Meals

Pasta

Ingredients

1 cup pasta
pinch salt
water

Method

In a bowl, add pasta and water to cover.

Bring to boil then simmer till tender.
3-9 minutes depending on pasta type.

In microwave for 3-7 minutes depending on pasta type.

Pasta Sauce

Ingredients

2-3 tomatoes sliced
2-3 mushrooms sliced
1 teaspoon garlic
1 onion sliced
1 teaspoon soya sauce
2 teaspoons sugar
1 tablespoon oil
2 teaspoons vinegar
salt and pepper to taste

Optional
Chilli flakes

Method

In a fry pan, add ingredients and fry till tender.

Add on top of pasta (see recipe above).

Rice

Ingredients	**Method**
½ cup rice pinch salt knob butter water	Rinse rice in cold water. Add all ingredients to a bowl, using enough water to cover the rice. Microwave on high for 3 minutes. Stir, Microwave 5-6 minutes till tender. Or boil on stove in saucepan for 6-10 minutes till tender.

Sausages/Chops, Eggs, Onions

Ingredients

2 sausages or chops
2 eggs
1 sliced onion
salt and pepper to taste
some oil for cooking in

Optional
Mixed Vegetables
Hash Browns
French Fries (Chips)
Sauce

Method

I go to the butchery or deli and ask for two sausages or a chop or two.

Put some oil in a fry pan and heat.

Add sausages or chop and sliced onion. Turn frequently so as not to burn.

Remove onions when ready and fry two eggs.

Combine on a plate and enjoy.

Fish Cakes

Ingredients

2-3 potatoes
1 teaspoon butter/margarine
1 small can salmon/tuna
1 egg
1 onion sliced and diced
1 tablespoons flour
salt pepper to taste

Optional
Parsley
vegetables

Method

Wash and clean potatoes, boil in a saucepan of water till cooked (8-10 minutes).

Or prick the potatoes cut into quarters and microwave for 3-5 minutes till cooked.

Drain, place in a bowl with a knob of butter and mash.

Add other ingredients and mix together, may need a dash of water to mix.

Put some oil in a fry pan, moderate heat, spoon mixture into cakes into fry pan and fry till golden brown both sides.

Creamed Corn Fritters

Ingredients

1 medium can creamed sweet corn
1 egg
salt and pepper to taste
¾ cup self-raising Flour

oil or butter for frying

Optional
Can also be instead of creamed corn.
Small tin tuna/salmon, diced ham/luncheon, bananas.

Method

Combine sweet corn and egg in a bowl. Mix in flour and beat until smooth. Season with salt and pepper.

Heat sufficient oil and butter in a frying pan to lightly cover the base.

Drop in batter from a table spoon and cook until brown on both sides.

Drain on kitchen paper and serve immediately.

Makes 10-12 fritters.

Poached Eggs

Ingredients

2 eggs
dash of vinegar
salt pepper to taste
parsley
2 slices toast

Method

In a fry pan or saucepan add about 50mm/2in of water and bring to the boil.

Add a dash of white vinegar to the water.

Crack an egg into the fry pan or saucepan.

Wait 3-4 minutes until cooked.

Remove with a slotted spoon or egg slice.

Place on some toast on a plate.

Add salt pepper, parsley to taste.

Toasted Sandwich

Ingredients

4 slices bread
2 eggs
grated cheese
butter/margarine

Optional:
Chopped tomato, onion, pineapple, bacon or tuna.

Can also use baked beans, spaghetti, creamed corn etc.

Method

Butter the bread.

Press the buttered side down into The Sandwich Maker. (I use one that goes on top of the gas ring).

Crack the eggs into the sandwiches.

Add as many optional ingredients as you want.

Put the next bread on top butter side up.

Trim the bread from the edges.

Cook till golden brown each side.

Vegetable, Fish/Meat Patties

Ingredients	**Method**
1 Potato	Cut raw vegetables into small cubes place into Kitchen Whiz and grate to much smaller pieces.
1 Kumara (Sweet Potato)	
1 Carrot	
1 onion	Or use a grater.
1 egg	
2 tablespoons self-raising flour	In a bowl add grated vegetables, meat or fish and other ingredients.
salt and pepper to taste	
1 tin small tuna,	
or salmon or some cooked beef, pork or chicken	Put some oil into a fry pan and heat.
cut into small pieces	
small amount oil.	Spoon tablespoon amounts into the fry pan.
	Fry the patties both sides.

Makes 10-12 Patties. This example with Beetroot.

Rice Risotto

Ingredients

½ cup rice
some oil
1 onion sliced
1 carrot sliced
½ red pepper de-seeded and sliced
½ green pepper de-seeded and sliced
2-3 mushrooms
2 tomatoes sliced
salt/pepper to taste
½ cup cooked meat or fish, chicken, ham etc.

optional
2 tablespoons Worcester sauce or soya sauce
some wine
some mixed vegetables.

Method

The preparation for risotto requires more simmering than boiling and one must be gentle in the cooking process.

In a fry pan add ½ cup water and rice, heat gently till cooked, make sure to keep water added and stir frequently.

When rice is cooked remove excess water. add some oil, soya sauce and other ingredients, cook till vegetables ready and heated through.

Tortellini (Pasta) and Fish

Ingredients

1 packet Ready to Serve Tortellini.

1 small tin tuna/salmon, or diced ham/luncheon, diced cooked chicken, beef or pork.
salt and pepper to taste

Method

place Tortellini and Fish on a plate.

Microwave for 1 minute. Stir before heating for another ½ to 1 minute.

Add salt and pepper and serve.

Tortellini and Tuna.

Creamy Mushrooms and Bacon on Pasta

Ingredients

1 onion, peeled and chopped
2-3 rashers bacon, sliced
½ medium sweet red pepper, de-seeded and chopped
½ medium green pepper, de-seeded and chopped
3-5 fresh mushrooms sliced
1 cup small pasta spirals
boiling salted water
some oil for fry pan

Sauce
¾ cup cream (or milk and 2 teaspoons cornflour)

Optional
1 teaspoon chopped fresh herbs
(parsley, basil, chives)
Fried Eggs

Method

Cook the onion, peppers and bacon in the oil in a hot fry pan, until the bacon is crispy and the onion lightly browned. Before fully cooked add mushrooms.

Mix the Sauce and add to the pan and heat through. Thicken the sauce, if necessary add more cornflour.

Meanwhile cook the pasta in boiling salted water for around 10 minutes until the pasta is al dente or just cooked.

Drain and put the pasta onto a plate.

Add the contents of the fry pan onto the plate.

Serve topped with fresh herbs.

Salmon Pasta Bake

Ingredients

1 medium tin salmon opened and drained
1 cup spiral pasta
1 onion, chopped
½ red pepper, de-seeded and sliced
½ green pepper, de-seeded and sliced
1 small carrot grated
¼ cup mayonnaise
1/3 cup cream
3-5 fresh mushrooms sliced

Optional
basil, oregano, parsley
½ cup cheese

Method

Cook the pasta in a saucepan of boiling salted water for around 10 minutes until the pasta is al dente or just cooked.

In a bowl with a little oil add mushrooms, onion, peppers, cook in microwave 2-3 minutes until tender.

Or in a fry pan with a little oil add mushrooms, onion, peppers, cook until tender.

In a bowl add salmon and broken into small pieces. Stir in other ingredients..

Cook uncovered in microwave for 3-5 minutes, stirring occasionally.

Or Cook uncovered in a dish and bake in an oven for 5-10 minutes, stirring occasionally.

Boil Up

Some Real East Coast Kai (food). This is real easy and a great feed.

It also allows to use not often used meat ingredients. Like pork bones, fish heads, tripe, pig trotters, pig head, bacon bones, mutton chops, sheep head, ox tails. Or any cheap off cuts of meat.

Ingredients

Meat of your choice (see above)
2 potatoes washed quartered
1 onion, peeled, chopped
1 carrot cleaned and sliced
portion of pumpkin sliced
portion of puha or watercress
1 kumara (sweet potato)

Optional
cabbage
bok choy
adjust quantities for more people

Method

Prepare all the ingredients and place in a large pot of boiling salted water.

Cook for and hour or more on low.

Would be excellent in a slow cooker..

Even better reheated the second day

Easy Meat Curry

Ingredients

1 onion
some garlic
1 teaspoon mixed spice
1 teaspoon sugar
2 tablespoons curry powder (more or less)
1 small tin apple sauce
1 small tin tomato purée
some chicken stock
½ cup milk
1 ½ cups cooked chicken

Optional
Meat could also be beef, pork or fish

Method

Fry onions, garlic, spices, sugar and curry powder, with a little oil.

Add remaining ingredients, stir well, heat and serve on a bed of rice.

I did a Chicken Curry, with onions, tomatoes, carrot.

Vegetable Curry

Ingredients

1 cauliflower, florets
2 carrots, sliced
½ green pepper, chopped
1 onion, chopped
some garlic
2 potatoes, washed, cubed
25g/1oz peas
1 teaspoon curry powder
1 teaspoon ground coriander
½ teaspoon turmeric
cream coconut, to taste
1 banana, sliced
some oil for cooking in

Method

Heat oil in a fry pan.

Fry onion and garlic, add coriander, turmeric, cauliflower, carrots, pepper and potatoes fry for a few minutes.

Add curry paste and 1 cup of water.

Cover and simmer for 15 minutes.

Add the coconut and banana, heat through.

Fresh coriander can be added at the end.

Serve with rice and naan bread.

Spanish Omelette

Ingredients

2 medium potatoes
3 eggs
2 tablespoons oil
1 onion sliced
salt and pepper to taste

Optional
Sauce

Method

Wash, slice and fry potatoes in a little oil in a fry pan.

Brown onions in the fry pan

Whisk eggs and salt and pepper in a bowl and add to the fry pan, flip the omelette when cooked on underside.

Spanish Omelette with tomato sauce.

Stir Fry

Ingredients

1 teaspoon oil
100g/4oz pork, beef, chicken cut into pieces
1 onion sliced
1 teaspoon cornflour
1 tablespoon soy sauce
1 tablespoon orange juice
50g/2oz vegetables, peas, carrots, beans
1 tomato sliced

Optional
rice or pasta
soya or Worcester sauce

Method

Mix meat, oil, onion in a bowl and microwave for 2 minutes, stir, microwave for 2 minutes or till cooked.

Blend in cornflour, soy sauce, orange juice.

microwave 2 minutes.

Stir in cooked vegetables microwave 1 minute.

Or put some oil in a fry pan, add mixture and heat till cooked.

Serve with rice or pasta or noodles.

This one is fresh fish, a tin of peas and carrots, a tomato and an onion.

Macaroni Salad

Ingredients

½ cups macaroni, cooked
2 tomatoes, diced
1 onion, diced
½ green pepper, diced
¼ cup cucumber, diced
¼ cup sugar
½ cup oil
1/3 cup tomato sauce/ketchup
¼ tsp. pepper
some paprika

Method

Cook the macaroni in a saucepan of hot water till soft.

Strain the macaroni and run cool water over it because you don't want hot macaroni.

Place macaroni in a large bowl with diced tomatoes, onions, green pepper, and cucumber.

In a large bowl, mix together the sugar, oil, sauce, pepper, and paprika.

Pour mixture into the other bowl with the macaroni.

Mix all together and then refrigerate.

Serve.

Potato Salad

Ingredients	**Method**

Ingredients

3 potatoes boiled
1 tin whole kernel corn, opened and drained
¼ cup chopped parsley
salt and pepper to taste
1 tablespoon French dressing
¼ cup mayonnaise

Optional
Tomato sliced
cheese grated
Spring onion
Boiled eggs
Carrot grated

Method

Put a Saucepan of water on the stove and boil, add the washed and halved potatoes and boil for 10-12 minutes till cooked.

When cooked drain the saucepan and cool the potatoes. Then dice the potatoes.

Mix all the ingredients in a salad bowl.

Tip
Make some mayonnaise, in the sauce section of this cook book.

Egg Toastie

Ingredients

2 slices bread
1 egg
margarine/butter to put on bread
1 slice of cheese
some Marmite
salt and pepper to taste
dash of oil

Optional
1 onion sliced

Method

Butter or margarine the outside of the bread.

Place slice cheese and other selected fillings between bread slices, butter side out.

Heat fry pan and cook both sides of toastie till golden brown.

Place on a plate.

Add a little oil and fry an egg.

Flip the egg and then add to the toastie.

Dagwood Sandwich

Ingredients	**Method**
2 slices bread	Choose your bread.
Meat, ham, luncheon, cooked chicken, corned beef etc.	Pick your selection of meats.
Boiled eggs peeled and sliced	
2 slices Cheese. (your favourite)	Select your cheese.
Vegetables, lettuce, red pepper sliced, tomato sliced, cucumber sliced, onion sliced, beetroot, radish sliced, mushrooms sliced.	Prepare the Vegetables.
Add Whatever takes your fancy the Skies the Limit	Assemble the basic food by layering on a slice of bread.
salt and pepper to taste	
1 tablespoons mayonnaise.	Layer your meat, vegetables and cheese in an alternating pattern for best taste.
Optional	
Tomato sauce, Mustard, horseradish pickle sliced	Add condiments.
Fish, tuna	Add the top slice of bread.
Bacon cooked	
Apple, kiwi fruit	If you wish and depending on the ingredients, microwave for 20-30 seconds or heat in a griller for a wee while.
Gherkins	
Olives	

Let your imagination run wild!

You can have as many ingredients and as large a sandwich as you want.

Bread Roll Beauties

Ingredients

bread rolls or 1 long French bread
2 tablespoons garlic butter
1 medium can baked beans or spaghetti opened
2 slices of ham or luncheon, diced
slices of cheese

Optional
1 cup cooked cubed chicken, beef or pork
soya or Worcester sauce

Method

Cut the rolls in half long ways on a chopping board.

Put the baked beans or spaghetti one half of the roll.

Dice the ham or luncheon and add to the bun.

Cut the cheese into strips and add to the bun.

Heat for a few minutes till heated in a microwave or griller.

Steak, Eggs, Chips

Ingredients

1 potato cleaned sliced thinly
2 eggs
1 steak
salt and pepper to taste
oil for fry pan

Optional
1 onion peeled, sliced
2 tomatoes sliced
½ green pepper, de-seeded and sliced
½ red pepper, de-seeded and sliced
mixed vegetables.
soya or Worcester sauce

Method

Add some oil to the fry pan and heat.

Add the potato slices flat in the pan and cook both sides.

Fry eggs and other desired vegetables.

Fry steak to your needs.

Serve on a plate.

Bill's Brew

Ingredients

1 potato cleaned sliced
1 onion peeled, sliced
2 tomatoes sliced
½ green pepper, de-seeded and sliced
½ red pepper, de-seeded and sliced
1 small tin salmon
salt and pepper to taste
oil for fry pan

Optional
mixed vegetables.
1 cup diced ham, cooked cubed chicken, beef or
pork
soya or Worcester sauce

Method

Add some oil to the fry pan and heat.

Add the potato slices flat in the pan and cook
both sides.

Gradually add other vegetables, cover and heat
for a few minutes till cooked.

Magic Bullet (Kitchen Whiz)

Also called a Blender or Food Processor.

Great machines, saves heaps of time, easy to clean.

Very easy meals and snacks.

Things you can do with a Magic Bullet (Kitchen Whiz)

You can find how to do all these recipes in the"10 Second Recipes" book that comes with the Magic Bullet when you buy it.

Chopping Onions and Garlic (no tears)
Smoothies (it makes the best smoothies!)
Frozen cocktails
Grinding Coffee Beans
Mixing Batters and Breads (example- when making muffins everyone can get their favourite blueberry, chocolate chop, or banana nut.)
Chopping Fresh Herbs
Grinding Spices
Grating Cheeses
Grinding Meats
Whipping Cream
Making Baby Food
Dips- (salsa, bean dip)
Stuffed Mushrooms
Pancakes
Omelets or Scrambled Eggs
Soups and Sandwiches

Chocolate Mousse

Ingredients	**Method**
¼ cup heavy cream (or just ordinary cream and 1-2 tablespoons of icing sugar)	Add ingredients to the Kitchen Whiz
2 table spoon Chocolate syrup	Whiz till mixed.

Thick Shake

Ingredients	**Method**
splash milk	Add ingredients to the Kitchen Whiz
1 ½ cups vanilla ice-cream	
chocolate syrup	Whiz till mixed.
Fruit blueberry, strawberry, banana	
small chocolate bar - MMs	

Smoothie

Ingredients

Fruit - Banana - berries - Peach – Nectarine etc.
1 cup milk
dash vanilla essence
1 egg
1-2 tablespoons Milk Flavouring like Nestle Nesquik

To sweeten add 1 tablespoons honey or maple syrup.

Method

Break or cut up fruit, add to the Kitchen Whiz, add other ingredients.

Whiz till mixed smoothly.

Egg Nog

Ingredients

3 eggs
2 tablespoons sugar
pinch of salt
1 ½ cups milk
½ tea spoon vanilla

optional
Shot of Rum

Method

Add ingredients to the Kitchen Whiz

Whiz till mixed.

Batter, Sauces, Dressings

Fish Batter

Ingredients	**Method**
1 tablespoon flour 1 egg 3 tablespoons milk pinch of salt	Mix in a bowl

Brown Sauce

Ingredients	**Method**
1 tablespoon oil 1 onion chopped 1 tablespoon flour 1 cup water 1 teaspoon Marmite/tomato sauce	Add oil into a fry pan, brown onion add flour brown lightly add water and Marmite/tomato sauce.

White Sauce

Ingredients	**Method**
30g butter 4 tablespoons flour 1 cup milk salt and pepper to taste some lemon juice can also add parsley, cheese, onion	Add butter into a fry pan heat, add other ingredients and simmer till cooked..

Tartare Sauce

Ingredients	**Method**
¼ cup Sour cream ½ cup Mayonnaise 2 gherkins, finely chopped 2 teaspoon lemon juice 1 tsp Lemon rind, finely grated	Combine all the ingredients, mix well and serve.

French Dressing

Ingredients

pinch salt
pepper to taste
4 tablespoons vinegar
4 tablespoons olive oil

Method

Mix ingredient in a bowl. Whisk till combined.

Mayonnaise

Ingredients

1 egg
1 teaspoon mustard
½ teaspoon salt
¼ teaspoon freshly ground white pepper
1½ teaspoons white wine vinegar
1 cup oil, peanut or corn
1 to 2 tablespoons lemon juice

Method

Place everything but the oil and lemon juice in the Kitchen Whiz container. Process 10 seconds in the whiz. Add the oil, whiz 10 seconds and then taste.

Add lemon juice to your taste.

If the mayonnaise is too thick, thin with hot water or lemon juice. If too thin, process a little longer.

Chocolate Icing

Ingredients

50g softened butter or margarine
1 cup icing sugar
2 tablespoons cocoa powder
2 tablespoons boiling water

Method

Beat butter and icing sugar together in a bowl.

Add cocoa and boiling water and beat until creamy.

Make rather thick for pouring onto cakes etc.

Lemon Icing

Ingredients

1 cup icing sugar
1 table spoon lemon juice

Method

Place icing sugar in heat proof bowl, add lemon juice. Stand over a pan of hot water until the mixture is smooth.

Pour quickly over the cake and if necessary spread with a knife dipped in hot water.

Custard

Ingredients

1 ½ cups milk
1/3 cup cream
½ tsp vanilla essence
4 eggs, yolks only
3 tablespoons caster sugar
2 level teaspoons cornflour

Optional
Apple sliced
Peaches
Fruit Salad
Pears
Nectarines etc.

Method

Add the milk, vanilla to a small bowl/saucepan, microwave 3 minutes on medium or bring up to simmering point slowly over a low heat on the stove. Try not to boil.

Whisk the yolks, sugar and cornflour together in a bowl until well blended.

Pour the hot milk and cream on to the eggs and sugar, whisking all the time with a balloon whisk.

Return to the bowl/pan, (add vanilla essence if using) and over a low heat microwave for 1 minute or in the saucepan gently stir until thickened.

Pour the custard into a jug and serve at once.

Serving suggestion, serve by pouring over some sliced apple. Add a little cream.

Other Recipes

Damper (Bread)

Ingredients

4 cups self-raising flour
1 teaspoon salt
30g 1oz butter
1 cup milk
½ cup water more or less

Method

Put flour and salt into large mixing bowl and rub in butter. Make a well in flour and pour in milk and water. Mix with a knife until the dough leaves the side of the bowl. Place on a greased scone tray and pat out until 20cm 8in in diameter.

Cut across on top and place in hot oven 220C 425F and bake for 25 minutes, lower heat to moderate 180C 250F and bake for a further 10-15 minutes or until the damper sound hollow when rapped with your knuckles.

Serve sliced with butter and golden syrup or jam.

Easy Bread

Ingredients

1 cup self-raising flour
1 egg
½ cup milk (enough to make mixture)
½ teaspoon salt
¼ teaspoon baking soda

Method

Mix the ingredients in a bowl.

Allow to sit for 10 minutes.

Heat a fry pan with a small amount of oil in it.

Add mixture and spread out to cover the bottom of the pan.

When it is cooked underneath, flip with an egg slice and leave till other side cooked.

Serve with butter and jam.

Easy and Cheap to make anywhere any time.

Simple Menu Ideas

Sausages eggs tomato chips
Fish eggs tomato chips
Steak eggs tomato chips
Rice Salmon fish sausages stew
Pasta Peas sardines/mackerel
Potatoes peas fish/stew/sausages
Fruit salad rice pudding
Porridge or wheat biscuits
Instant pudding and fruit
Pikelets
Scones
Fish cakes
Toasted sandwiches with baked beans, spaghetti, sweet corn, eggs, cheese onion pineapple
Sandwiches fish/cheese/eggs
Poached eggs with fish/sardines
Sweet Corn fritters
Omelette cheese, fish, ham, mushrooms
French Toast
Pancakes with golden syrup or honey
Salad with ham/luncheon
Bacon and Eggs, Tomatoes, Chips, Onions
Baked Beans on Toast
Bread Pudding
Instant Popcorn
Bacon and Eggs
Frozen precooked meal cooked in microwave
Instant Noodles and toast
Dagwood sandwich

etc.

Notes

Notes

Alphabetical Index

The Simple On The Road Cook Book

A Useful Easy, Simple and Budget Conscious Guide for Bachelors and
other Food Preparation and Cooking Challenged People.
Especially if Living in a Confined Space or On The Road.

Copies of this book can be ordered from
www.lulu.com/leftfieldnz

or
Bill Rosoman
PO Box 4155
Hamilton East 3247
New Zealand
www.creativekiwis.com

ISBN 978-0-473-16684-7

Made in the USA
Monee, IL
07 July 2026